How Places Got Their Names

How Places Got Their Names

Graham Rickard

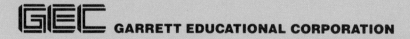

GARRETT EDUCATIONAL CORPORATION

PICTURE ACKNOWLEDGMENTS

Australian Information Services, London 11, 30; BBC Hulton Picture Library 8, 16, 21, 33, 40, 44; Bettmann Archive/BBC Hulton Picture Library 28; Florida Dept. of Commerce, Division of Tourism 41; Gibraltar Dept. of Tourism 17; Illustrated London News 32, 37; Mississippi Dept. of Tourism 23; National Film Board of Canada 39; New Zealand National Publicity Studios 13; Pakistan Embassy 12; private collection 18; SATOUR title page, 7, 15; Texas Tourist Development Agency 14, 27, 35; Tunisian National Tourist Office 43; U.S. Travel and Tourism Administration 19, 22, 31, 38, 42; Utah Travel Council 36; Venezuelan Embassy 10; Zimbabwe Tourist Board 25.

The cover picture shows Sir Walter Raleigh ordering the standard of Queen Elizabeth to be raised on the coast of Virginia (private collection).

The picture on the title page shows a reconstruction of the Great Trek of 1836-1838 during the Centenary Celebrations in Pretoria, South Africa (SATOUR).

Text © copyright 1989 by Garrett Educational Corporation
First published in the United States in 1989 by
Garrett Educational Corporation, 130 East 13th Street,
Ada, OK 74820
First published by Young Library Ltd., Brighton, England
© Copyright 1985 Young Library Ltd.

Manufactured in the United States of America

Library of Congress Cataloging in Publication Data

Rickard, Graham.
  How places got their names / Graham Rickard.
    p. cm.
  Includes index.
  Summary: Presents the stories behind the naming of seventy places all over the world, from Adelaide and Africa to Washington and Zimbabwe.
    1. Toponymy—Juvenile literature.   [1. Names, Geographical.]
I. Title.
G100.5.R53   1989   89-12022
910'.014—dc20   CIP
  ISBN 0-944483-34-8   AC

CONTENTS

Adelaide	23	Colombia	40	New Jersey	13
Africa	43	Colorado	19	New South Wales	6
Alexandria	6	Dallas	25	New Zealand	12
Alice Springs	36	Dead Sea	23	Oklahoma	42
Amazon	34	Falkland Islands	26	Pacific Ocean	18
America	14	Florida	32	Pakistan	12
Argentina	33	Gibraltar	17	Pennsylvania	28
Atlantic Ocean	31	Greenland	24	Philadelphia	21
Australia	30	Houston	35	Phoenix	12
Bath	18	Hudson Bay	33	Red Sea	9
Bering Sea and		Ivory Coast	24	Rio de Janeiro	8
Bering Straits	29	Johannesburg	15	Rome	9
Black Sea	20	Kimberley	16	St. Lawrence	34
Bolivia	16	Ladysmith	21	St. Louis	10
Brazil	40	Lake Victoria	44	Salt Lake City	36
Budapest	34	Llanfair P.G.	15	San Francisco	38
Buenos Aires	31	Los Angeles	29	Society Islands	20
California	31	Mackenzie River	17	Tasmania	11
Canada	44	Maryland	24	Texas	26
Canary Islands	34	Memphis	6	Toronto	26
Cape of Good Hope	10	Miami	41	Vancouver	39
Carolina, North		Mississippi	23	Venezuela	10
and South	20	Montevideo	42	Virginia	16
Chicago	22	Montreal	9	Washington	8
China	37	Mount Everest	29	Zimbabwe	25
Christmas Island	26	Natal	7	*Index*	45

Memphis

Nineteenth-century Americans were proud of their achievements in developing the continent, and liked to compare their society to those of ancient Egypt, Greece, and Rome. Many places in the United States are named after places of ancient civilizations. The Mississippi River was often described as "the Nile of America," and people hoped for great civilizations to spring up along its banks. When a town was founded at the river's junction with the Ohio it was, naturally, named Cairo.

In 1826 a second new town was laid out farther down the river. Its founder was Andrew Jackson, president of the United States, 1829-1837, and he named the town Memphis. Memphis was another ancient city on the Nile; its name means "place of good abode." If the city's founder did hope to recreate the wealth and splendors of the ancient East, he was not disappointed. Memphis grew to be an important port for the cotton trade, and the largest city in the state of Tennessee.

Alexandria

Alexander the Great founded the city which bears his name after invading Egypt in 332 B.C. A few months after marking out his city on the shore of the Mediterranean, he left Egypt, never to return until his body was brought back to Alexandria for burial.

Alexander would have been proud of the fact that Alexandria was, for over 1,000 years, the center of Mediterranean culture. Greeks, Romans, Jews, and Christians in turn built libraries, universities, temples, and palaces here. The famous lighthouse on the island of Pharos was regarded as one of the Seven Wonders of the World. Cleopatra courted Julius Caesar in the city. Cleopatra's Needle, the stone obelisk that now stands on London's Embankment, came from Alexandria. Alexandria is still one of the Mediterranean's major ports and an important naval base.

New South Wales

On August 12, 1770, Captain James Cook was sailing past a strip of Australian coastline near Port Macquarie. It reminded him of the coast of South Wales, and when he took possession of the territory he named it New Wales. He was usually a talented namer of his discoveries, but he later made this unimaginative name even more cumbersome when he changed it to New South Wales.

When first colonized by Britain, New South Wales included modern Queensland, Victoria, South Australia, Tasmania, and even New Zealand.

Natal

For many years Portuguese sailors had been venturing farther and farther south down the west coast of Africa. They wanted to see if India could be reached by sea, by sailing around the vast African continent. In 1487 Bartolomew Diaz had discovered that a way around Africa did exist.

So, on July 8, 1497, Vasco da Gama sailed from Portugal on a historic mission to reach India. Three months and 4,000 miles later, da Gama rounded the Cape of Good Hope at the southern tip of the African continent. The storms of the South Atlantic had taken a terrible toll on his ships, and he landed at Mossel Bay to carry out repairs. The expedition sailed on until Christmas Day, then landed at a spot da Gama named Terro do Natal. "Natal" is the Portuguese word for "Christmas Day." He did finally reach India, and returned laden with spices and precious stones — but at a terrible cost. During the two years of his journey, more than three-quarters of his 170 men died, mainly from scurvy. Natal is now one of the four provinces of the Republic of South Africa.

A wagon breaks down in mid-river as early pioneers open up the territory of Natal.

Washington

The first president of the United States gave his name to the country's capital city.

After the American War of Independence, Washington was a natural choice for anyone looking for a place name. As well as being the hero of the war, George Washington had become the country's first president. Any American who opposed honoring him with a placename was immediately accused of being unpatriotic. The chaotic result is that more than 200 districts, counties, villages, and towns in the United States share the name of Washington. Of all these, only the nation's capital in the District of Columbia, on the Potomac River between Maryland and Virginia, grew to be of any great size.

However, the situation was further confused in 1853 when the territory of Washington was founded in the far northwest of the country, on the Pacific coast. In 1889 it became a state. If you wish to send a letter to the capital of the United States, make sure you add "D.C." (District of Columbia) to the name.

Rio de Janeiro

This famous Brazilian seaport was given its name as the result of a mistake by Portuguese sailors in 1502. The sailors were part of an expedition led by Amerigo

8

Vespucci (who later gave his own name to the entire continent of America). When they sighted the large bay where the city now stands, they mistakenly thought it to be the estuary of a great river. As it was the first day of January, they named this nonexistent river Rio de Janeiro, meaning "January River." Despite its inappropriateness, the name was retained when the city was founded in 1566.

Rome

Legend tells us that Rome was founded by the twin brothers Romulus and Remus in the eighth century B.C. When they were born their great-uncle Amulius ordered them to be drowned in the River Tiber. The container in which they were thrown into the river floated downstream. It came to rest on a bank, where the children were found by a she-wolf and a woodpecker.

Romulus and Remus were nursed and fed by these animals until they were discovered by Faustulus, a herdsman. He and his wife brought them up until their royal blood was recognized. Then they killed Amulius and placed their grandfather on the throne.

They decided to build a town on the site where the wolf found them. Afterwards they quarreled, and Remus was killed. The city was named Rome after Romulus, and he became the first king of a civilization that was eventually to grow into the vast Roman Empire.

The Red Sea

The Red Sea lies between Africa and Arabia. Since the days of the ancient Greeks it has always had the same name. The water has a reddish tinge, caused by brightly colored shells and coral beneath its surface. This is the most obvious reason for its name, but there are at least three other possibilities. Its sandy banks are also red. Parts of the coast were once inhabited by a tribe called the Himarites, whose name also means "red." Many Asian and African cultures used color names to indicate directions, and Red Sea meant "south sea."

Montreal

Jacques Cartier, a French navigator, was the first European to make voyages of discovery up the St. Lawrence River in Canada. He made three voyages between 1534 and 1541. On the first of these he discovered an extinct volcano, and named it Mont Royal ("Royal Mountain") in honor of his king.

Later, when French settlers established the city on the mountain's slope, they named it Ville-Marie (Marytown) in honor of the Virgin Mary. However, the name was soon changed to a version of Cartier's original Mont Royal. Today Montreal is the second largest city in Canada.

Cape of Good Hope

For many years Portuguese sailors had been exploring the western coast of Africa. They had been penetrating farther and farther south in an attempt to find a sea route round the vast continent to India. At last, in 1487, Bartolomew Diaz was the first European to reach the southernmost point of the continent and sail around it into the Indian Ocean.

Diaz did not see the coast on his outward journey, but on the return journey he sailed through terrible storms before he finally sighted the tip of the continent. He therefore named it Cabo Tormentoso (Cape of Storms). However, King John of Portugal was worried that other explorers might be put off by this name, so he changed it to Cabo de Boa Esperanca — the Cape of Good Hope.

Diaz had good reason for his original name. Twelve years later he was drowned off the Cape when his ship went down in a storm.

The shore of Lake Maracaibo, where Indian villages reminded European discoverers of Venice.

into the bottom. Communication from one house to another is by canoe."

The village reminded the explorers of Venice, so they named it Venezuela, which means "Little Venice." The name of this one small village soon spread to include the whole surrounding area, and in 1830 it became the official name of the entire country.

Venezuela

In the late fifteenth century the Spaniards were exploring and colonizing in the South American continent. In 1499 an expedition led by Alonso de Hojeda came to the shores of Lake Maracaibo, and found an Indian village built out over the water on wooden piles. Hojeda was impressed, and wrote, "Its houses are built ingeniously in the water, supported on stakes driven

St. Louis

In 1763 the Seven Years War came to an end, and France and Britain finally stopped fighting over their American territories. Britain was in possession of all the land to the east of the Mississippi River. Many of the French settlers who lived on the river's east bank hated the idea of English rule. Under the leadership of Pierre Laclède they decided to set up a new settlement on the other side of the river. Laclède selected a site "to establish

This is what one of New[...] city and port — Wellingt[...] 1840.

In 1642 the Dutc[...] Tasman sighted parts o[...] called it Staten Lanc[...] current name for the[...] continent. Tasman tl[...] he saw could be part[...] The name was later [...] geographers to Nieuw[...] of the Dutch province[...] could not call it Nieu[...] that was their name f[...] time.

The name became[...] Zealand as the early[...] whale hunters, were n[...]

a settlement which might hereafter become one of the finest cities in America."

The name St. Louis was chosen because it was in the Louisiana Territory, and the reigning French king was Louis XV. But to these patriotic Frenchmen, the name also honored a far greater king, Louis IX, who had ruled France 500 years earlier. He was the ideal medieval king, a great soldier, and a lover of beauty, who was made a saint after he died fighting the Saracens on a crusade.

Tasmania

The first European discoverer of this large island on Australia's south coast was the Dutch navigator Abel Tasman, in 1642.

Tasmania's capital city, Hobart. Tasmania changed its name from that of one Dutchman to another.

He named it Van Diemen's Land, after Antony van Diemen, who was the governor-general of the Dutch East Indies Company. Tasman had no idea that it was an island, nor did anyone else until 1798. The name lasted for 200 years, and the island became notorious as a penal colony for British criminals who were brought there from England.

When its use for criminals ended in 1853, the island wanted to improve its image. It was felt that "diemen" sounded too much like "demon." Unofficially the islanders were already using the name of the man who had discovered it, in the poetic-sounding form of Tasmania.

Pakist

In 1947 India was gi
and ceased to be part
pire. Most of India f
religion, and the Mus
to form a separate st
they would otherwise k
vast Hindu majorit
agreed to their dema
this new state to be ca

The chosen nam
devised by a group of
Cambridge Universit
letters from the name
Punjab, **Afghanista**
Sind, and Baluchis**TA**
cidence, the name in
also means "land of

Pakistan was created f
one of the beautiful m
possesses.

America

In 1492 Christopher Columbus, an Italian navigator in the service of Spain, set sail on a historic voyage across the Atlantic Ocean. He was looking for a westward route to the Orient. When he sighted land he was convinced he had reached Asia. Even though he made two further trips, he went to his death still believing he had reached only the eastern shores of Asia.

In 1499 another Italian navigator was commissioned by the king of Spain to explore the lands Columbus had seen. His name was Amerigo Vespucci. He sighted land near Nicaragua, and sailed around the Gulf of Mexico before returning to Spain. In 1501 he made a further trip to the coast of Brazil. Vespucci was the first to realize that he had found a great continent — a "new world."

In 1507 a German map publisher produced his *Cosmographiae Intruductio*. It included a description of the new lands by Vespucci, and also a picture of him, and it suggested that the New World be named after him. Amerigo became America. If it had not been for Amerigo Vespucci, perhaps America would now be known as Columbia.

Not a typical scene any more, but it still happens — cattle being driven through a town.

Johannesburg

When gold was discovered in the Witwatersrand area of the Transvaal in South Africa, it started a massive epidemic of "gold fever." Thousands of prospectors flooded into the area in the hope of making a quick fortune. They threw up an untidy cluster of corrugated-iron shanties and named it after Johànnes Meyer, the country's first mining commissioner. He would not have been very flattered because Johannesburg in those early days was a wild place, with many drinking and gambling halls, and the riotous atmosphere of America's Wild West. It was a place to make a fortune as quickly as possible, and then get out.

But within fifty years this sordid collection of tents and tin huts grew into the busy streets and fine buildings of South Africa's greatest city. The Witwatersrand goldfield proved to be one of the biggest in the world, and today Johannesburg is still the center of the world's gold-mining industry.

In fifty years Johannesburg grew into the center of the world's gold-mining industry.

Llanfairpwllgwyngyllgogerychwyrndrobwllllantysiliogogogoch

With fifty-eight letters, this village in Anglesey, in North Wales, easily wins the title of the longest place name in Britain. Translated from Welsh, it means "St. Mary's Church in the hollow of the white hazel trees near the rapid whirlpool and the church of St. Tysilio near the red cave." The official name consists only of the first twenty letters. However, during the nineteenth century, the name was extended to become the longest in Wales in order to attract tourists. It is often abbreviated to Llanfair P.G., but the full name was used on the platform sign when the railway station was reopened in 1973.

Welsh people count only fifty-one letters in the full name, because in the Welsh language "ll" and "ch" are single letters.

Simón Bolívar liberated several countries from Spanish rule, and gave his name to one of them.

Bolivia

In the sixteenth century the Spanish conquered and colonized most of Central and South America. One of the colonies was the New Kingdom of Granada in the northwest of South America. In 1821 it became independent of Spain after an eleven-year war.

Simón Bolívar, known as the Liberator, was the great hero of this struggle for independence. He became president and military dictator of Great Columbia, which at this time included Panama, Ecuador, and Venezuela.

In 1822 Bolívar was invited by the colony of Upper Peru to lead their fight for independence. He drove out the Spaniards after two years of fighting, and the country changed its name to Bolivia in his honor.

Virginia

In 1584 Queen Elizabeth I gave Sir Walter Raleigh a grant to settle the lands in the New World. He sent two of his captains to explore possible sites, and when they returned he took their reports to his queen. They wrote of a rich, sweet-smelling land on the Atlantic coast, ruled by a chief called Wingina. The queen was struck by this name. She herself was known as "the Virgin Queen," and the name of Wingina seemed similar. Putting her thoughts into a Latinized form, she came up with the name Virginia, which was duly written on the map.

It was the first name that the English gave to America, and the site of the first permanent colony in 1607. In 1789 Virginia was the most populous and wealthy of the thirteen colonies that were formed into the United States of America.

Kimberley

In 1866 a farmer near the Orange River in South Africa saw his friend's children playing with a bright shiny stone which they had found lying on the ground. He had it examined, and immediately started the great South African "diamond rush."

All the surrounding farms were bought up by hopeful mining companies, which then leased sites to prospectors for small monthly fees.

In 1870, prospectors found an amazing "pipe," the richest source of diamonds in the world, and people of every class and nationality poured into the area. These new settlers founded a makeshift town and named it after Lord Kimberley, the English Colonial Secretary at the time. It was built on the farm where that first diamond was discovered. One writer described its strange mixture of inhabitants as "a marvellous motley assemblage, among whom money flows like water from the amazing productiveness of the mine."

The famous Rock of Gibraltar, which guards the entrance to the Mediterranean Sea.

Gibraltar

"The Rock," at the southern tip of Spain, has for thousands of years guarded the entrance to the Mediterranean Sea. For ancient civilizations it formed the limits of the known world, and was a meeting point for the two great cultures of Europe and Africa. In A.D. 711 Muslim Arab forces, under Tarik ibn Zaid, crossed the sea from Africa and captured the rocky promontory. He built a fortress here and named it "Geb-al-Tarik," meaning "the mountain of Tarik." When the Spanish reclaimed the territory, the name stuck, although in a slightly different form.

The rock was later taken by Britain in 1704, during the wars of the Spanish Succession. It has remained an important British naval base ever since. The Spanish have consistently tried to reclaim it, but an overwhelming majority of the Gibraltar population prefer continued association with Britain.

Mackenzie River

The Athabasca River flows for more than 600 miles from the Rocky Mountains into Lake Athabasca. The next portion, known as the Slave River, flows 240 miles into the Great Slave Lake. From there it flows more than 1,000 miles into the

Arctic Ocean, and takes its name from the man who discovered and navigated it.

Alexander Mackenzie was born in Scotland and came to America at the age of ten. He wanted to be the first man to cross the American continent to the Pacific Ocean, and hoped that the lower portion of the Athabasca would lead him there. In 1789 he set off downriver, but after several weeks realized with disappointment that it was carrying him north, not west. He reached the Arctic Ocean in July, bitterly disappointed.

Three years later he set off again westwards and this time succeeded in reaching the Pacific after nine months of arduous travel. Proudly he wrote, on a rock in Puget Sound, "Alex Mackenzie. From Canada by land 22nd July 1793."

A group of fashionable ladies and gentlemen driving from London to Bath in a steam carriage.

was used for both bathing and drinking, and royalty and aristocracy came to the spa to "take the waters." The water gained a reputation for curing many ailments. No bathing is allowed there these days, but it is still possible to buy glasses of water to drink.

Bath

This city is built on the site of the only natural hot-water springs in Britain. The ancient Romans were very fond of bathing, and were delighted to discover the warm springs in this cold northern province of their empire. They built a city called Aquae Sulis, but by A.D. 796 the name had changed to Bathum, which was later shortened to Bath.

In the eighteenth century, Bath was rediscovered by the fashionable aristocracy, and Beau Nash transformed it into a summer playground for London's high society. The water, at 49°C (120°F),

Pacific Ocean

The first European to sight the world's largest ocean was the Spanish explorer Vasco Balboa. He reached it in 1513 after marching across the Panama isthmus, and named it South Sea.

Seven years later, the great Portuguese navigator Ferdinand Magellan sailed around the South American continent, in an attempt to reach the Spice Islands. He threaded through the strait which now bears his name, and entered onto the mighty ocean. Because he enjoyed such fine weather on the three-month crossing, he named it Mar Pacifico — calm sea. "Pacifico" it has remained, of which the English version is Pacific.

Colorado

The Colorado River was given its name by the Spaniard Don Juan de Oñate in 1604. The word in Spanish means "red," and the waters are reddish with clay washed down from canyons. The river is formed by the union of the Grand and Green rivers.

When the state of Colorado was formed in 1876, there was a lot of argument over what to call it. The general area lacked any established name. However, there was a tradition of naming states after rivers, and so the name Colorado was adopted.

More than half a century later it was realized with embarrassment that the Colorado River did not in fact flow through the state of Colorado! However, one of its headwaters — the Grand River — *was* in the state. So, rather than change the name of the state, they decided to change the name of the river, and the Grand became the Colorado in 1921.

Tourists admiring the ancient cliff houses of the Indians of Mesa Verde, Colorado.

North Carolina and South Carolina

"Carolus" is the Latin form of Charles, and the two states of Carolina in the United States are named after three different kings of that name.

A French colonizer, Jean Ribaut, first established a settlement of Huguenots here in 1560, and named it La Caroline after the French King Charles IX. The settlement did not last long, and the name fell out of use. In 1629 the territory was granted to an Englishman, Sir Robert Heath. He also named it Carolina, after his king, Charles I. In 1663, the state was regranted to a group of nine owners. They kept the name of Carolina in honor of their king, Charles II, for whom the name was, of course, equally suitable.

Society Islands

The Society Islands are a group of islands in the South Pacific, a part of French Polynesia. The largest of these islands is Tahiti. In 1769 the British navigator, Captain James Cook, took a party of scientists to these islands. They wished to observe the passage of Venus across the sun, in an attempt to calculate the distance between the sun and the earth. The trip was organized by the Royal Society in London, and Cook named the islands in honor of the Society.

However, they could easily have been named after the friendly "society-loving" people who lived there. This South Sea paradise had previously been visited by Samuel Wallis, and his sailors were captivated by the beautiful women on the islands. The natives were still living in a Stone Age culture when he arrived, and any metal objects were highly prized. It did not take the sailors long to discover that a single nail would buy an evening's pleasure. In his report, Wallis wrote: "Every cleat in the ship was drawn, and all the nails carried off . . . Most of the hammock nails were drawn and two-thirds of the men obliged to lie on the deck for want of nails to hang their hammocks."

Black Sea

Iranian-speaking tribes were the first to inhabit the shores of the Black Sea. Noting the difference between the water of their inland lakes and that of the open sea, they called it Axsaena, meaning "dark." When the ancient Greeks came to the area, they first called it merely Pontius (meaning "sea") but later adapted the Iranian name as Axeinos, which means "inhospitable." This was later changed to Euxeinos, which means "hospitable!" Perhaps they thought the sea would respond kindly to the new name.

But the idea of inhospitability stuck. There are sudden bad storms in the Black Sea, and little shelter for ships on its coasts. It was probably the Turks who therefore gave it the name by which we call it today.

Philadelphia

The English Quaker, William Penn, founded Pennsylvania in the seventeenth century as a haven of tolerance for persecuted religious minorities. He wanted this state to have a grand capital city, with a name which suited the dignity and high ideals on which it was founded. He chose the name Philadelphia, a city mentioned in the Bible, because its name in Greek means "brotherly love." Penn later wrote, "And thou, Philadelphia, the virgin settlement of this province, named before thou wert born, what care, what travail has there been to bring thee forth!"

Penn laid out the city's streets on a grid pattern, and was the first to name them after numbers — First Street, Second Street, and so on. This practice was copied by many other U.S. cities.

Ladysmith

Sir Harry Smith was a British soldier who became a national hero in 1834 when 12,000 Hottentot tribesmen swept across the border into Cape Colony in South Africa. Smith made a famous six-day ride from Cape Town to Grahamstown to take command of the army.

After service in India, during which he led the charge against the Sikhs at Aliwal, Smith returned to Africa in 1847 as governor of Cape Colony. During the five years that he was governor he was a dashing, impetuous figure who never let anyone stand in his way. In 1848 he declared British sovereignty over all the land between the Orange and Vaal rivers. Twelve hun-

Ladysmith was the site of a famous siege during the Second Boer War, 1899-1902.

Chicago celebrates an occasion with a colorful display of flags, bands, and floats.

dred Boers who tried to resist him were routed by his well-disciplined force of 850 men, and they were forced to accept his authority.

The town of Ladysmith was named in honor of Smith's Spanish wife. Three other towns in Africa commemorate his life — Harrismith, Whittlesey (his native town in England), and Aliwal.

Chicago

One of America's largest cities has a right to be proud about many things, but certainly not its name! It comes from an Algonquian Indian word, meaning "stinking." It stands beside the waters of Lake Michigan. Here the wild garlic grew in tremendous profusion, and the local skunks were hunted for their fur. In 1688 a Frenchman wrote, "We arrived at a place called Chicagou which . . . has taken this name from the amount of garlic growing wild in that vicinity." Because the water smelled so bad, many jokes were made about the town, which was often referred to as "Skunk-town," or worse.

Understandably, the name was never popular with the inhabitants. When the present city was formally founded in 1803 it was named Fort Dearborn after the American Secretary of War, Henry Dearborn. The name was never properly adopted, however, and Chicago has been the official name since 1830.

Adelaide

Many of Australia's towns were named to commemorate English monarchs or statesmen, most of whom had no interest whatsoever in the country, except as a convenient dumping ground for convicts. Many British people emigrated there, especially after convict transportation ended. In 1836 the town of Adelaide was founded in South Australia. It was named at the personal request of the king, William IV, after his German wife, Adelaide. The new town prospered and came to be the capital of the state of South Australia, but never had any other connections with Queen Adelaide.

Dead Sea

The Dead Sea is not really a sea but a large inland lake. The River Jordan flows into it, and there is no outlet to the ocean. The water evaporates constantly in the great heat, leaving the salts behind, and its salt content is therefore so high that very little organic life can survive in its waters. That is why it is called the Dead Sea. Another effect of the high salt content is that the water is very buoyant. It is impossible for a swimmer to sink.

The Dead Sea is one of the world's most famous inland waters in history, and there are references to it dating back thousands of years. It lies partly in Israel and partly in Jordan. Both countries use it as a source of salt, and as a popular holiday attraction.

Mississippi

The Mississippi is a great American river flowing from northern Minnesota 2,470 miles (3,974 km) south to the Gulf of Mexico. Together with the Missouri it is the third longest river in the world. Mississippi is also the name of the state bounded on its western border by the river.

As early as 1659 a French explorer priest in Canada wrote that Indians had given reports of "a beautiful river, large, wide, deep, and worthy of comparison, they say, with the St. Lawrence." Seven years later another priest wrote of "the great river named Messipi," although no Frenchman had yet been there. The Algonquian Indians called it Missi-Sipi. Somewhat to our disappointment, we learn that this intriguing-sounding name

A modern version of the beautiful old paddle steamers which used to ply the Mississippi.

means simply "great river." Throughout the world there are many examples of the same name in different languages. The Rio Grande, Yukon, Zambesi, and the Ta Ho in China, all mean Great River. However, none is as memorable (or as difficult to spell) as Mississippi.

Ivory Coast

For hundreds of years after discovering Africa, Europeans had no real interest in the continent except as a rich source of gold, jewels, and slaves. They rarely bothered to explore inland, and named various sections of the coastline after the most important trading goods — such as Grain Coast, Gold Coast, Slave Coast, and Diamond Coast. The hinterland of the Ivory Coast was very rich in wildlife, including elephants with their ivory tusks. Ivory was a very highly prized material, and was used by the rich of Europe for piano keys, billiard balls, combs, and cutlery handles.

The name may have had a more somber meaning, however. "Black ivory" used to be a common term for slaves among the traders in human flesh. Ivory Coast is now an independent nation of West Africa.

Maryland

In 1632 the English baron Cecil Calvert, Lord Baltimore, was given a grant of land to the north of Virginia. He wanted to establish a new colony there. This land included parts of present-day Pennsylvania and Delaware. Baltimore wanted to call it Crescentia, as he wished the colony to be known as one which was in crescent (growing). He knew Charles I's interest in giving names, however, and tactfully left a blank space when he drew up a draft of his charter.

The king had already given names honoring himself, his mother, and his sister. This time his thoughts naturally turned to his wife, Queen Henrietta Maria. When he suggested Mariana, Baltimore reminded him that this was the name of a Jesuit priest who had written against the monarchy. Baltimore was about to suggest Crescentia when the king announced that the new colony would be called Terra Mariae — Latin for Land of Mary. It was the fashion in the sixteenth and seventeenth centuries to give Latin names to colonies, but these names soon became anglicized with use.

Greenland

Around A.D. 986, a fiery-tempered Norseman called Eric the Red killed several of his farmer neighbors after years of violent quarrels. Outlawed from his native Iceland, he set sail westwards with his friends and family, looking for new lands to settle in, until a large landmass blocked his way. Because the world was going through a phase of warm weather, the southern tip of the land was richly covered in grass, so he named it Greenland.

But there was another reason. Eric wanted to colonize the land and attract settlers there. The saga which tells of his journey records that he named it Greenland "because men would more readily go there if the country had a good name." Eric's son Leif later discovered the eastern coast of America and named it Vinland. The history of the world could have been very different if he had not failed in his attempts to start a colony there.

Dallas

Dallas is now much better remembered for the death of a president (John Kennedy was shot here in 1963) than for the vice-president it was named for. Yet this otherwise forgotten vice-president is honored by a larger city than any president except Washington.

George Mifflin Dallas came from a well-off family in Philadelphia. He started the career of a gentleman-politician after attending Princeton University. He soon became a senator, minister to Russia and Great Britain, and was vice-president 1845-1849. In 1846 Texas created and named a county after him. The new county town was also called Dallas. It is doubtful if the vice-president had ever even heard of the place. He would hardly have been flattered by his association with what was then a raw and dusty village.

Zimbabwe

The origin of the ancient stone ruins in Mashonaland, Zimbabwe, is one of Africa's greatest mysteries. They were

A corner of the stone ruins of Zimbabwe, whose origin is a mystery.

built in the Middle Ages, with huge granite walls, centuries before any other stone buildings in southern Africa. They were probably built by Bantu people, but could have been constructed by early traders from Arabia or India. The name means "stone houses" and was adopted by the black African national movements that were fighting to overthrow the country's white government in the days when the country was called Rhodesia.

In 1980 Rhodesia became an independent nation, and its name was officially changed to Zimbabwe. The country's national fish-eagle emblem was taken from a carving found in the ancient ruins.

Toronto

The city of Toronto is built on the shore of Lake Ontario, and its name records the importance of the lake in the city's history. The area was once thickly forested, and the Iroquois Indians who lived here made use of the lake for moving the timber they needed for their houses, boats, and fuel. The Iroquois name for the area was Toron-to-hen, meaning "timber in the water."

The French built a fort here in 1749. The British later founded a town on the same site and named it York, in honor of King George III's son, the Duke of York. However, when Toronto was officially made a city in 1834, it reverted to a form of the Indian name.

An alternative belief is that the name comes from a Huron Indian word meaning "place of meeting."

Falkland Islands

The English sea-captain John Davis first discovered these cold, bleak islands in the South Atlantic, and named them Davis Land. Two years later, Sir Richard Hawkins renamed them Hawkins Maidenland, in honor of Elizabeth I, "the Maiden Queen." It was in 1690 that Captain John Strong gave them their present name, in honor of Viscount Falkland, Charles I's chief Minister of State, who had financed Strong's expedition.

They have been British territory for most of their history, but are also claimed by Argentina, where they are called the Malvinas. This argument developed into warfare in 1982 when the Argentinians invaded the islands but were repulsed.

Christmas Island

This island is part of the largest coral atoll in the Pacific. It was "discovered" twice, each time at Christmas, so its name is well deserved.

Captain William Mynors was the first European to discover it, on Christmas Day 1643, but it was then lost and forgotten for over a hundred years. On December 24, 1777, Captain James Cook landed here and gave the island its name "because we kept our Christmas here." However, the island's connections with Christmas ideals of peace and goodwill towards men were shattered in 1957 when it was used as a testing ground for hydrogen bombs.

Texas

The state of Texas is bordered on the south by the country of Mexico and on the southeast by the Gulf of Mexico.

A cowboy hard at work in the Palo Duro Canyon of the Texas Panhandle.

There is some confusion about the origin of its name. In 1690 a Spanish monk called Damian landed on the coast and met a group of Indians. When he asked which tribe they belonged to, they excitedly repeated the word "texia." Damian wrote the word not realizing that in fact it was a greeting, meaning "friend." However, the confusion had started six years earlier, when seven Indians came to the Spanish governor at El Paso to ask for missionaries and help in a war. They spoke of "the great kingdoms of Texas," so perhaps to some Indians it *was* the place name.

In 1691 a Spanish expedition arrived at a village to be greeted with the words "Techas! Techas!" (Friends! Friends!) They realized that it was a greeting rather than the name of a tribe, but Spanish officials had already started using the name Texas in their reports.

Pennsylvania

This name was the result of a royal joke at the expense of the sedate Quaker, William Penn.

William Penn was the son of the British admiral Sir William Penn. He was converted to Quakerism at an early age, and suffered much persecution. He was imprisoned several times but refused to give up his beliefs. In 1681 King Charles II granted him a territory of land in the New World, to the west of the Delaware River, as payment for a debt the king owed to Penn's family. When Penn went to receive his charter from the king, he proposed the name New Wales, because the territory was said to be as hilly as Wales. But when the charter was handed to him it bore the name Pennsylvania (the Latin word "sylvania" means forest land). Charles II knew that Quakers were against all forms of egotism and vanity, and the name was the result of the king's sense of humor.

Penn's protests and bribes were in vain, and to his intense embarrassment the name became permanent. He later tried to explain away the king's joke by saying the

William Penn is greeted by the settlers of the American colony named after him.

28

name was in honor of his father, or that it was from the celtic word "pen," meaning headland.

Mount Everest

The world's highest mountain lies on the border of Nepal with Tibet, in the Himalayan range. The official height of the mountain is 29,028 feet (8,848 meters), but this is slowly increasing all the time because the entire Himalayan range is still rising. The summit was first reached by the New Zealander Edmund Hillary and the Nepalese Tensing Norgay in the British expedition of 1953.

The original Tibetan name Chomolungma ("mother goddess of the earth") would probably be more suitable than the one by which it is known today. It is named in honor of Sir George Everest, the English surveyor-general of India. He was a bureaucrat rather than a man of action, and newspapers of the time commented that he had "more to do with papers than with mountains."

Bering Sea and Bering Straits

In the early eighteenth century, no one was sure whether Asia and America were part of the same continent, or separated by the sea. Peter the Great of Russia hired the Danish captain Vitus Bering to solve the question.

Leaving from Kamchatka, Bering sailed along the southern Siberian coast until he could see no land to the north or east. He returned to Russia having proved that the Asian and American continents were divided by a strait.

He set sail again in 1740, to explore the sea between the two continents and survey the north coast of Siberia. He reached the Alaskan coast and explored the Aleutian Islands. But after a few months he and many of his crew were ill with scurvy. They decided to spend the winter on an island, but he died there in December 1741. It was not until the nineteenth century that the strait was named after him, together with the sea to the south of it and the island on which he died.

Russia claimed Alaska until 1867, when Tsar Alexander II sold it to the United States for 7,250,000 dollars (12 dollars per square mile).

Los Angeles

Los Angeles is the largest city on America's West Coast. In 1781 the area was still part of Mexico. Spanish missionaries who settled here gave it the grand name of El Pueblo de Nuestra Señora la Reina de Los Angeles de Porciúncula, which means "The Town of Our Lady Queen of the Angels of the Little Portion." (The "little portion" was the piece of land which Benedictine monks gave to St. Francis of Assisi, and the city was founded on the Feast of the Porciúncula, which celebrates this event).

For obvious reasons the name was soon shortened to Los Angeles (The Angels). It remained Mexican until 1846, when it was attacked and taken by an American naval force. In 1850 it was formally annexed as part of the United States. Today the name is often shortened even further, to L.A.!

Australia

Geographers had guessed at the existence of a southern continent for many centuries before it was actually discovered.

In the second century A.D., Ptolemy published his *Geography*. It showed a vast area of the southern ocean as the continent of Terra Australis Incognita, which means "unknown southern land." This name was later shortened to Terra Australis, although it was still unknown. Dutch navigators were the first Europeans to sight the western and northern coasts of the unknown continent, and named it New Holland, but they had no idea how far it extended east and south.

The largest port in western Australia is named after Captain John Fremantle, an English navigator.

In 1768 the British navigator James Cook landed on the eastern coast of New Holland. In 1795 another Englishman, Matthew Flinders, reached New Holland. He decided it should revert to its old name of Terra Australis. This time the name stuck, although it was eventually changed to Australia.

Atlantic Ocean

The Ancient Greeks believed that there used to exist a vast island, in the ocean beyond Gibraltar, called Atlantis. This island had sunk down into the sea, taking its civilization with it. Many people today believe the Atlantic Ocean to be named after this fabulous land.

But another Greek myth offers a different explanation. Atlas, one of the Titans who took part in the war against Zeus, was condemned to hold aloft the heavens "at the western extremity of the earth, where day and night meet." Greek sailors, who rarely ventured outside the Mediterranean, believed this to be just beyond Gibraltar. Thus Atlas gave his name to the ocean around him.

You may choose whichever theory you prefer!

Visitors stroll down the main street of Calico, a ghost town in southern California.

women, and overflowing with gold and pearls. The island is called California.

No one is sure how this fictional island gave its name to the state on America's West Coast. Some people believe Cortes named it as a joke. On hearing a detailed description of the country's beauties, he called it California, and the name stuck before he could change it. This is probably just as much a myth as the Esplandian story itself. Probably an unknown explorer associated the fine country he saw with the fabulous land described in "The Exploits of Esplandian."

California

A popular Spanish romance called "The Exploits of Esplandian" was published in the sixteenth century. It mentions a fabulous island, populated entirely by

Buenos Aires

In Spanish, Buenos Aires means "good winds," but the origin of the name has nothing to do with the local weather. Buenos Aires, lying on the southern bank of the Rio de la Plata, is the capital of Argentina. Spanish settlers founded the city in 1535, and named it Ciudad de la Santisima Trinidad y Puerto de Nuestra Señora la Virgen Maria de los Buenos Aires, which means "City of the Most Holy Trinity and Port of Our Lady the Virgin Mary of Good Winds."

The first part of this name was given because the city was founded on Trinity Sunday; the second part because the Virgin Mary was the patron of sailors, who prayed she would send favorable winds for their ships. By the nineteenth century, it was understandably shortened to two words.

A nineteenth-century view of Buenos Aires, named after the patron saint of sailors.

Florida

Juan Ponce de Leon was the Spanish governor of eastern Hispaniola and Puerto Rico. Twenty years after the New World was discovered he sailed east with three ships, "to win honor and increase estate." It is believed that, being in bad health, he was also seeking the mythical "fountain of perpetual youth." In 1513, on the weekend after Easter, he saw land ahead and anchored offshore.

Ponce de Leon thought it was an island, never realized it was part of the mainland, and was impatient to name it at once. It was Easter, which in Spanish is called Pascua de Flores. Also, the land was richly covered with trees and flowers, and the Spanish term for a field of flowers is

"florido." For these two reasons de Leon named it Florida. It is the oldest European name in America.

Argentina

In 1526 the English explorer Sebastian Cabot was employed by King Charles of Spain to explore and map the South American coastline. Hearing rumors of great mineral wealth, he began exploring the rivers. At the mouth of the River Paraná he bought gold and silver from the Indians and sent it back to Spain. This gave the area a reputation for great wealth.

The Paraná and Uruguay rivers together form an estuary. Cabot named this estuary Rio de la Plata (Silver River) because of the silver he had obtained in the area. Three hundred years later a huge Spanish colony in South America achieved independence. On its northeastern border lay the Rio de la Plata. The new country decided to keep the idea of "silver" in its name. "Argent " is Latin for silvery, so the country became Argentina.

Hudson Bay

Very soon after discovering the American continent, Europeans began to look for a way around it, to reach the Orient by sailing west. They tried to sail around it to the north, and named the route the Northwest Passage hundreds of years before they actually found it!

Among those who braved the icy waters

Henry Hudson was cast adrift by a mutinous crew in the bay now named after him.

of the far north was the English explorer Henry Hudson. After three unsuccessful attempts he sailed from London in 1610, and finally entered what is now known as the Hudson Straits. He explored Hudson Bay, a huge gulf, where his ship was ice-bound for the entire winter. In spring, when the ice had melted, he wanted to continue, but the harsh winter had proved too much for his crew. They mutinied, and Hudson and his young son were cast adrift in a small boat to die. Nothing is known of their fate.

Today he is remembered not only by Hudson Bay but by the Hudson River, on which New York City stands, and by more than twenty other places on the American continent.

Amazon

In Greek legend, the Amazons were a tribe of female warriors who made slaves of their male prisoners.

In 1541 the Spanish explorer Francisco de Orellana made the first descent down the river, from the Andes to the Atlantic. He reported that he and his men were attacked by tribes of savage female warriors, and hence named the river "Amazonas." The king of Spain granted Orellana the right to take possession of the country, but he lost his ships on the way out. It is said that he died of grief.

An alternative explanation is that the river's name derives from "amossona," an Indian word for "destroyer of boats," because navigation on the river is endangered by floods, rapids, and tidal waves.

The Amazon is the longest river in the world at 4,195 miles (6,750 km). Its Atlantic estuary is 150 miles wide, and it turns the sea water from salt to brackish for over a hundred miles from the shore.

Budapest

Budapest, the capital city of Hungary, was once two separate towns divided by the Danube River. Buda, on the hilly west bank of the river, was the site of a Roman camp and later became the royal residence. After the Mongol invasion of 1241 it developed as a center of agriculture and rural crafts.

Pest, on the opposite side of the river, was involved in commerce and new industries. The two towns continued their separate lives until 1872, when they merged their names and Budapest became one great city. Today the two halves are joined by six road bridges, two railway bridges, and an underground railway tunnel.

St. Lawrence

In 1535 the French explorer Jacques Cartier (who also gave Montreal its name) ran into a bad storm as he was sailing along the Canadian coastline. He managed to find refuge in a small bay on August 7, and gratefully named it after St. Lawrence, whose feast day it was.

He returned the following year to explore the whole area. What began as the name of a small bay grew to cover the whole gulf and the great river which now divides Canada from the United States.

Canary Islands

Canaries live in the wild on this group of islands off the northwest coast of Africa. However, the birds are named after the islands. The islands are not named after birds, but after dogs!

In ancient times the islands were visited by Greeks and Romans. They named them Insulae Fortunatae, the Fortunate Islands, because of the wonderful climate.

Later the islands were forgotten and were not rediscovered until 1334, when a French ship was driven among them by a storm.

When a Spanish expedition landed here in 1402, they had heard rumors of wild men with dogs' heads, and when they heard barking, they named the islands Islas Canarias, meaning Dog Islands. When they found not dog-men, but pretty sweet-singing birds, they too were called canaries. The canary birds were more fortunate than the people who inhabited the islands. The people were cruelly persecuted and have long since died out. The birds remain, however, to delight us with their beautiful song.

Houston

Today's great "Space City" is founded on the site of a battle which won Texas its independence from Mexico. The commander of the Texan forces was Samuel Houston, an extraordinary man who had been adopted by a Cherokee Indian in Tennessee. He rose to be governor of Tennessee, but in 1829 he abandoned his bride, his office, and his friends and spent three years among the Cherokees before going to Texas.

The skyscrapers of "Space City" still allow room for a reminder of its colonial past.

On the banks of the San Jacinto River, Houston inflicted a crushing defeat on the Mexican forces. After the battle, a town was laid out on the site, and its builders patriotically and gratefully remembered their general by naming it Houston.

Salt Lake City

The Mormons, or Latter-Day Saints, are a religious organization founded in America in 1830 by Joseph Smith.

Many people quickly accepted Smith's beliefs, but his followers were persecuted by their fellow Americans, and Smith himself was eventually murdered by his opponents. To escape further persecution, one of his "disciples," Brigham Young, gathered the Mormons together,

The monument to the Mormon leader Brigham Young, in Salt Lake City.

and like Moses led them into a wilderness. They wandered into the Rocky Mountains looking for a place to settle, until Young stood on a mountainside near the Great Salt Lake. He declared "this is the place," and they built a city near its banks.

This spiritual refuge was meant to be a heaven on earth, and Young originally named it New Jerusalem. But the other Mormon leaders, fearing further persecution, decided that it should be called the City of the Great Salt Lake. The city is still the center of the Mormon faith, which today has over two million followers.

Alice Springs

Until the nineteenth century, Australia's major coastal towns were separated by the vast and inhospitable central area of desert and bushland. Communication between them was almost impossible. Then in 1870-1872 Sir Charles Todd built a telegraph line right across the continent, from north to south — a distance of some 1,800 miles. On March 11, 1871, an exploring party led by surveyor W. W. Mills, seeking a wagon route for supplies, came across a grassy basin with a pool of clear water. He named it in honor of Sir Charles Todd's wife.

What started as a lonely telegraph post in the center of the outback grew into a thriving town, especially after the discovery of opals near there. Later a railway connected it to Adelaide in the south, and the Stuart Highway was built from Alice Springs to Darwin in the north.

China

China, the most heavily populated country in the world, has never had a name which its people used to cover the whole country. "China" is a name used only by foreigners. About 200 B.C. the Ch'in dynasty managed, for a short while, to unite all the territories into one empire. Indians who traded with them for silk and spices therefore began to use the name Chin. The name passed into Greek and Roman, but with the first letter changed to "s," so we still have such terms as

A section of the Great Wall of China, completed in the third century B.C., *which is 1,400 miles long.*

"sinologist" (a specialist in Chinese affairs) and 'Sino-American relations."

In the sixteenth century Europeans added the final letter to the Indian name and gave us "China." But it still remains a foreign name, and the Chinese themselves have struggled for centuries to find a suitable name for the country. "The Flowery Kingdom" and "Middle Kingdom" have both been recent unsuccessful attempts.

San Francisco

A confusing historical tangle lies behind the name of this famous California city, and it all revolves around the name "Francis." Sir Francis Drake started it all in 1578, when he named a nearby bay Port St. Francis. Some twenty years later a Portuguese explorer, Sebastian Rodriguez Cermeño, found a good harbor farther up the Californian coast. There was a Franciscan friar on board who was named Francisco, and he named the bay San Francisco.

So two explorers named Francis had

Cable cars, still used today, were introduced in the nineteenth century on San Francisco's steep hills.

named separate bays after the same St. Francis, but neither was what we now call San Francisco. That was not discovered by Europeans until 200 years later. In 1776 Franciscan monks were searching for Cermeño's bay, where they wanted to found a mission. Instead, they found a much larger bay thirty miles to the south and mistakenly called it San Francisco. When they realized their mistake, they renamed the smaller bay Drake's Bay.

The confusion continued for some

time, and the present city did not officially adopt the name until 1847. It had a population then of about 2,000, but has since grown to be one of the largest cities in the United States.

The city and island of Vancouver, named after a British navigator of the eighteenth century.

Vancouver

George Vancouver joined the navy as a lad of thirteen, and worked his way up through the ranks before joining Captain Cook's expedition as a midshipman. In 1792 he was appointed to chart Canada's western coastline, and arrived at a large island off the coast of British Columbia. It had been discovered exactly 200 years earlier by the Spanish navigator Juan de Fuca, whose name is given to the strait at the island's southern end. As well as being an outstanding seaman, Vancouver was fortunately also a very good diplomat. Although he had to take possession of the territory, he and the Spanish governor of the area became firm friends. He tactfully suggested that the island should have two names — Quadra and Vancouver. Governor Quadra agreed, but the Spanish name was soon forgotten.

On the mainland, opposite the island, the Hudson's Bay Company founded a settlement in 1825. This town, also, was named after Captain Vancouver. It became the terminus of the Canadian Pacific Railway in 1887 and the largest city in western Canada.

Colombia

The present republic of Colombia is in northwest South America. It is almost as big as Britain, France, and Spain together, but used to be even bigger. In 1536 the Spanish established the New Kingdom of Granada. In 1810 the colony became independent and at that time covered all of present-day Venezuela, and Ecuador as well. Twenty years later the different parts of the country broke away. Not until 1861 did the country come to be called Colombia.

The great soldier Simón Bolívar wanted a new name for his republic. As Christopher Columbus had visited that coast in 1502, Bolívar chose Colombia as the name. A great many places on the American continent are named after Columbus. In the nineteenth century there was a strong movement in the United States to rename the whole country after Columbus, but Bolívar had beaten them to it.

Christopher Columbus gave his name to Colombia and to hundreds of other places in the New World.

Brazil

Brazil was discovered in the year 1500 by the Portuguese admiral Pedro Alvares Cabral. He first sighted the coast on May 3, the feast of the Finding of the True Cross. Therefore he promptly named the territory Terra de Vera Cruz, which means "Land of the True Cross." However, this name did not last very long. In 1503 an expedition discovered brazilwood trees, from which a red dye called braza could be extracted. It was this which gave the new country its present name.

But for many years before Cabral, sailors had spoken of the legendary island of Brasil. It was said to exist somewhere

in the Atlantic, and this ancient myth could easily have played a part in naming this new country.

The city of Miami, mysteriously named from an Indian language not spoken in this part of America.

Miami

Miami is a strange name. There are five Miamis in the United States, but they all mean different things. They come from separate, unrelated Indian languages, but there is no word like it in the local Seminole Indian language.

In Ohio, the Mayami were an Indian tribe who gave their name to several places. Early European settlers in Ohio took the name with them when they moved to Florida. So the name of the most famous Miami has no local meaning at all. Until 1895, as a tiny hamlet, it was known as Fort Dallas, but the name changed after the coming of the railroad brought enormous expansion.

41

Montevideo

In 1519 Ferdinand Magellan, the Portuguese navigator, set off on his historic attempt to reach the Spice Islands by sailing westwards. After crossing the Atlantic he turned south along the coast of South America, looking for a route around the continent. In the following year he was sailing past the coast of Uruguay, which is mainly flat and lacking in landmarks. The lookout suddenly sighted a hill (the 480-foot cone-shaped Cerro), and shouted in his excitement, "Monte vidi eo!," which in Portuguese means "I saw a mountain!." Glad for a break in the monotony, Magellan named the spot with the sailor's words.

A fort was built on the Cerro in 1717 and the first settlement of the town was made in 1726. In 1828 it became the capital of the newly formed republic of Uruguay.

Oklahoma

This American state gained its name as the result of some quick thinking by a defeated Indian chief after the American Civil War of 1861-1865. Five great Indian tribes had made the mistake of fighting on the losing side, by allying themselves with the Confederates. After their defeat, it was decided to punish them by taking away some of their tribal lands, and a delegation of chiefs was summoned to Washington in 1866. Among these was the well-educated chief of the Choctaws, the Rev. Allen Wright. The Choctaws had no real name for their lands, but when asked the name of his territory, Wright quickly replied "Oklahoma," which in Choctaw means simply "red-skinned people." His lands may have been taken by the white man, but the chief's name made it clear to whom they really belonged.

It was intended that the ceded territory should be reserved for settlement only by other Indian tribes, but white settlers moved in, and it was eventually admitted to the Union as a state in 1907.

The impressive Pioneer Woman statue which stands proudly in Ponca City, Oklahoma.

Africa

It was the Romans who named Africa. Here is one of their amphitheaters in the ancient city of Carthage.

The ancient Greeks named this huge continent Libya. Libya later came to mean the northern part between Egypt and Ethiopia and the Atlantic; and later still, the present-day republic lying between Egypt and Algeria.

The ancient Romans thought of Africa as an extension of Europe. It was one small Berber tribe, the Afrigs, who eventually gave their name to the whole continent. The Afrigs took their name from the Arabic word "afira," meaning "to be dusty." When the Romans conquered the area in the second century B.C., they named their new province "Land of the Afrigs" — Africa. The name stuck, and as new territories were explored over the centuries, the name gradually spread south to cover the whole continent.

Another possibility is that the name originally applied to a fertile area of present-day Tunisia, named Ifriqiyah, which in Arabic means "ears of corn."

43

Canada

Ships arriving in Montreal in 1762. Today it has become the second largest city in Canada.

The first great explorer of Canada was Jacques Cartier. Between 1534 and 1541 he made three voyages of discovery to the American continent. While sailing up the St. Lawrence River, Cartier used to ask the Indians what their villages were called. They always answered "Kanata" (which means settlement). This made Cartier assume it was the name of the entire country. With a small modification, this is what it became in 1867.

But not without disagreement. When it became time for the various colonies to unite under one government, some extraordinary names were proposed. They included Albionora, Borealia, Cabotia, Elfisga, Hochelaga, Norland, Superior, Transatlantia, Tuponia, and Victoria-land.

Lake Victoria

In 1856 Richard Burton and John Speke determined to discover the source of the longest river in the world — the Nile. From the East African coast they trekked inland for 900 miles until they reached Lake Tanganyika. Speke then carried on for another 200 miles north and found another great lake, which he named Victoria, after the British queen.

Burton and Speke argued bitterly about which of these lakes was the source of the Nile. Burton insisted it was Tanganyika; Speke argued that it was Victoria. Speke was proved correct, but not until after his death.

INDEX

Entries under countries include references to their activities in other parts of the world.

A

Adelaide 23
Africa 7, 10, 17, 21, 24, 25, 34-35, 43, 44
Alaska 29
Albania, America 13
Aleutian Islands 29
Alexander the Great 6
Alexandria 6
Alice Springs 36
Aliwal 22
Amazon River 34
America 6, 8, 10, 12, 13, 14, 16, 20, 22, 23, 25, 26, 28, 29, 31, 32, 38, 40, 42
American Civil War 42
Anglesey 15
Aotearoa 12
Argentina 26, 32, 33
Arizona 12
Athabasca River 17
Atlantic Ocean 31
Atlantis 31
Australia 6, 11, 23, 29, 36

B

Balboa, Vasco 18
Bath 18
Bering Sea and Straits 29
Bering, Vitus 29
Black Sea 20
Boer War 21
Bolívar, Simón 16, 40
Bolivia 16
Brazil 8, 14, 40-41
Britain 6, 10, 11, 12, 13, 15, 16, 18, 20, 21, 26, 31, 33
British Columbia 39
Budapest 34
Buenos Aires 31-32
Burton, Richard 44

C

Cabot, Sebastian 33
Cabral, Pedro 40
Cairo, Illinois 6

Calico, California 31
California 31, 38
Calvert, Cecil, Lord Baltimore 24
Canada 9, 17-18, 26, 34, 39, 44
Canary Islands 34-35
Cape Colony 21
Cape of Good Hope 7, 10
Carolina 20
Carteret, Sir George 13
Cartier, Jacques 9, 34, 44
Cermeño, Sebastian 38
Charles I, King of England 20, 24
Charles II, King of England 20, 28
Charles IX, King of France 20
Chicago 22
China 37
Christmas 7, 26
Christmas Island 26
Colorado 19
Colorado River 19
Colombia 40
Columbia, District of 8
Columbus, Christopher 14, 40
Cook, Captain James 6, 20, 26, 31
Cortes, Hernando 31

D

da Gama, Vasco 7
Dallas 25
Dallas, George Mifflin 25
Davis, Captain John 26
Dead Sea 23
Delaware 24
Delaware River 13, 28
Diaz, Bartolomew 7, 10
Diemen, Antony van 11
Drake's Bay 38
Drake, Sir Francis 38

E

Easter 32
Ecuador 16, 40
Elizabeth I, Queen of England 16, 26

Elizabeth, New Jersey 13
English Civil War 13
Eric the Red 24

F

Falkland Islands 26
Flinders, Captain Matthew 31
Florida 32-33, 41
Fort Dallas 41
France 9, 10, 20, 22, 26, 34
Fremantle 30
Fuca, Juan de 39

G

Gibraltar 17
Grand River 19
Greece 6, 20, 31, 43
Greenland 24-25
Green River 19
Gulf of Mexico 14, 23

H

Harrismith 22
Hawkins, Sir Richard 26
Hobart 11
Hojeda, Alonso de 10
Holland 11, 30
Houston 35-36
Houston, Samuel 35-36
Hudson Bay 33
Hudson, Henry 33
Hudson River 13, 33
Hungary 34

I

India 7, 10, 12, 37
Indians, of the American continent 10, 12, 16, 19, 22, 23, 26, 27, 33, 35, 41, 42, 44
Italy 14
Ivory Coast 24

J

Jackson, Andrew, president of the United States 6

Jersey 13
Johannesburg 15
John, King of Portugal 10

K
Kimberley 16-17

L
Laclède, Pierre 10
Ladysmith 21
Lake Maracaibo 10
Lake Ontario 26
Leif Ericson 25
Leon, Juan Ponce de 32
Libya 43
Llanfair P.G. 15
Los Angeles 29
Louis IX, King of France 11
Louis XV, King of France 11
Louisiana Territory 11

M
Mackenzie, Alexander 18
Mackenzie River 17, 18
Magellan, Ferdinand 18, 42
Maoris 12
Maryland 24
Memphis, Tennessee 6
Mesa Verde 19
Mexico 29, 35
Meyer, Johannes 15
Miami 41
Minnesota 23
Mississippi River 6, 10, 23-24
Montevideo 42
Montreal 9, 44
Mormons 36
Mossel Bay 7
Mount Everest 29
Mynors, Captain William 26

N
Natal 7
Netherlands, *see* Holland
New Holland 30
New Jersey 13
New South Wales 6
New Zealand 6, 12-13
Nicaragua 14
Nile River 44
Northwest Passage 33

O
Ohio 41
Oklahoma 42
Oñate, Don Juan de 19
Orange River 16
Orellana, Francisco de 34

P
Pacific Ocean 18
Pakistan 12
Panama 16, 18
Paraná River 33
Pennsylvania 24, 28-29
Penn, William 21, 28
Philadelphia 21
Phoenix 12
Ponca City 42
Portugal 7, 8, 10, 18, 38, 40, 42
Potomac River 8
Ptolemy the cartographer 30
Puget Sound 18

R
Raleigh, Sir Walter 16
Red Sea 9
Ribaut, Jean 20
Rio de Janeiro 8-9
Rio de la Plata 32, 33
Rome, Roman Empire 9, 18, 43
Russia 29

S
St. Lawrence River 9, 34, 44
St. Louis 10-11
Salt Lake City 36
Salt River 12
San Francisco 38
San Jacinto River 36
Seven Years War 10
Slave River 17
Smith, Joseph 36
Smith, Sir Harry 21
Society Islands 20
South Africa 7, 15, 16, 21
South America 8, 10, 14, 16, 18, 32-32, 33, 40, 42
Spain 10, 14, 16, 17, 18, 19, 26, 29, 31, 32, 33, 34, 35, 40
Speke, John 44
Spice Islands 18, 42

Strong, Captain John 26
Swilling, Jack 12

T
Tasman, Abel 11, 13
Tasmania 6, 11
Tennessee 6, 35
Texas 25, 26-27, 35
Tiber River 9
Toronto 26
Transvaal 15
Tunisia 43
Turkey 20

U
United States 16, 34, 39, 40, 41, 42, *see also* America
Uruguay 42
Uruguay River 33

V
Vancouver 39-40
Vancouver, George 39-40
Van Diemen's Land 11
Venezuela 10, 16, 40
Venice 10
Vespucci, Amerigo 8, 14
Victoria, Australia 6
Victoria, Lake 44
Victoria, Queen of England 44
Vinland 25
Virginia 16
Virgin Mary 9, 32

W
Wales 15
Wallis, Samuel 20
Washington, D.C. 8
Washington, George 8
Washington, state of 8
Wellington 13
Whittlesey 22
Wingina 16
Witwatersrand 15
Wright, Rev. Allen 42

Y
York, Duke of 26
Young, Brigham 36

Z
Zimbabwe 25

$14.95

$14.95

910 **Rickard, Graham**
RIC **How places got their**
names

DATE DUE	BORROWER'S NAME	
10/95	Chris Calhoun	T-10
12-16-	ELED	24

910 **Rickard, Graham**
RIC **How places got their**
names